DATE DUE			

DEMCO 38-297

SURFING

SURFING

by Jerolyn Nentl

Library of Congress Catalog Card Number: 78-8723

International Standard Book Numbers:
0-913940-93-3 Library Bound
0-89686-014-0

Edited by - Dr. Howard Schroeder
         Prof. in Reading and Language Arts
         Dept. of Elementary Education
         Mankato State University

Library of Congress
Cataloging in Publication Data

Nentl, Jerolyn Ann
  Surfing.

  (Funseekers)
  1. Surfing--Juvenile literature. I. Title.
GV840.S8N46   797.1'72   78-8723
ISBN 0-913940-93-3

Our special thanks goes out to Steve Pezman of Surfer Publications and Mike
Moir who supplied most of the photos used to illustrate this book.

Photo Credits
Surfer Publications: 14, 20A, 28
Mike Moir: 5, 6, 8, 11, 12, 13, 16, 18, 20B, 23A, 23B, 25B, 27, 30
Focus On Sports: Cover, 2, 25A, 26, 32
Women's International Surfing Association: 24
Pete Hornby: 29

SURFING

Riding the waves!

Everything is blue. Skip looks up and sees a brilliant blue sky. All around him is the blue of the endless ocean. He is floating gently back and forth, bobbing up and down, up and down. He is kneeling on a board in the Pacific Ocean waiting for a wave. Skip is a surfer and the board he is kneeling on is a surfboard. Suddenly, he sees a good wave approaching! He starts paddling his board to catch it. Quickly, he stands up. His feet are spread and his arms are out to help balance himself. He is riding the waves!

Surfing looks easy to the people watching from the shore. Those who ride the waves will tell you it is a rugged sport.

A surfer does not need to be big or strong to ride the waves. What is needed is good balance and muscle control. A good sense of timing and rhythm are also necessary. A good surfer rides with the wave like a good dancer sways to the music.

A person must be willing to work to be a good surfer.

Surfers must practice. They must spend long hours riding the waves again and again. There is no team to work with them. There is no coach to correct mistakes. There is no partner to help. Surfers are alone with their boards and the powerful ocean.

There is no one right way to surf. There are as many different ways to surf as there are surfers. This is true since the surf is never the same. It is different in different places. It is even different in the same place at different times of the day and year.

There is also no one type of surfboard. Surfboards come in many shapes and lengths. A surfer must consider his height and weight when buying a board. He must also consider the type of waves he wants to ride.

A lonely surfer watches the calm sea.

Surfers used to shape their boards by hand. Some were made from a single piece of wood. Old boards have been found in Hawaii that are 18 feet long and weigh 160 pounds! Today's boards are only about 10 feet long and are lightweight. Some of today's boards are made of wood strips glued together. Others are made of fiberglass or moulded foam. All are covered with a coating of plastic to help keep out the ocean water. Surfers rub wax on their boards so their feet won't slip.

The front of a surfboard is called the "nose." The rear is called the "tail." The sides of the surfboard are the "rails." The piece sticking down beneath the water is the "fin" or "skeg." It makes a board more stable by keeping the tail of the board in touch with the water.

Each surfer must change the way he surfs to fit the type of wave he is riding and the kind of board he is using. He must know a lot about the waves.

Most good surfers today are men. The surfing movie "Gidget" encouraged women to try the sport a few years ago. Today we find more women becoming interested in the sport than at any other time.

The surfboard comes in many sizes and shapes. Each board has the same basic parts as shown in the diagram below.

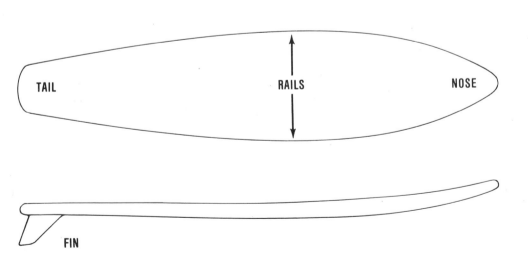

Surfers ride their boards anytime there is a good wave. It can be in the summer or the winter. It can be in the morning or at night. Most good waves seem to come at mid-day. The biggest come during the winter storms. A skin-diving suit, or "wet-suit," lets surfers ride these big waves in the cold, winter weather and still keep warm.

Most surfers in the United States live in Southern California. There are some surfers on the East Coast who ride the waves of the Atlantic Ocean. Some also ride the waves in the Gulf of Mexico. The surf in these areas is not as large as that of the Pacific Ocean. There are also many surfers in Australia. People in Mexico, South Africa, Puerto Rico, South America and Japan are discovering the fun of riding the waves, too!

Surfers ride the waves anytime day or night.

A wet-suit is used in cold water conditions.

Most surfers are found in Hawaii.

The sport of surfing started in Hawaii. It used to be one of the rarest sports in the world. Only the Polynesian kings and their chiefs surfed. The Hawaiians have often been called "the iron men of the sea."

Some say surfing is more than 400 years old. There were surfers in Hawaii in 1778 when Captain Cook discovered the islands. Some historians say surfing was part of the religious life of the Hawaiians in ancient times. Special prayers were said as a tree was chopped down. More prayers were said as a board was carved from the tree. Other prayers were said when it was launched in the water. Sometimes the water was even blessed.

Duke Kahanamoku.

Missionaries preaching the Christian religion came to Hawaii soon after Captain Cook. They discouraged surfing. They said the Hawaiians should wear clothes to cover their bodies to please the Christian God. It was hard to surf wearing lots of clothes!

People began to feel free enough to start surfing again by the 1900's. Many tourists were beginning to visit Hawaii, and liked to watch the surfers. When they went home to their own countries, they told other people about surfing. People started surfing in the United States about 1908.

No one knows exactly how surfing started. Perhaps someone stood on the shore one day and watched a storm wash ashore a piece of driftwood. Maybe someone got in trouble while swimming in the big waves and climbed on a piece of driftwood to save himself.

Whatever it was, the urge to conquer the waves has been with mankind for a long time.

One special Hawaiian is considered the Father of Surfing. He is Paoa Kahanamoku, or "Duke." He rode the waves for 62 years, until he died in 1967.

"Duke" Kahanamoku was the man responsible for introducing surfing to Australia. He first rode the waves there about 1915.

Surfers spend a lot of time waiting for those waves.

Surfers like "Duke" Kahanamoku are the experts. They have learned much about:

- the ocean and its waves
- beaches
- winds
- surfboards.

The ocean is never really still, not even for a moment. Waves are being created in the middle of the ocean at all times. The size and shape of a wave changes with the wind, the depth of the water, the ocean currents and the distance it travels before it reaches the shore.

Sometimes when there is no wind there are no waves. These are called "flat days."

The tide also affects surfers. There are better waves to ride at either high or low tide. Surfing at high tide gives a smoother ride. Low tide surfing gives a longer ride.

Waves come in three basic shapes:

- waves that cream at the top

- waves that curl just a little

- waves that curl so much they form a tube or cylinder.

Each type of wave provides a different kind of thrill. The size of the wave, from crest to trough, is not really important. It does not show how difficult that wave will be to ride. The shape of a wave is more important in deciding how much of a challenge it will be.

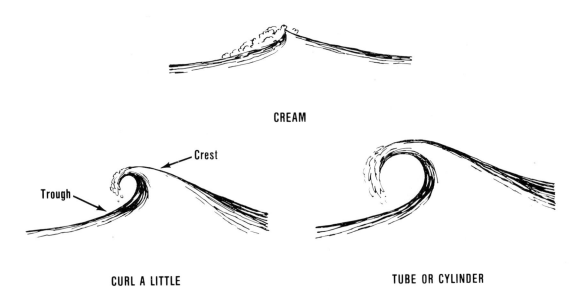

CREAM

CURL A LITTLE

TUBE OR CYLINDER

17

Almost any beach can be a good surfing spot if a surfer is there on a good day. Good waves do not always roll in on the same beach. This is the reason why most surfers try to predict the waves. Some day computers may help with this type of forecasting. Weather can be watched just by looking at the sky and the ocean. It can be watched by pilots flying high in the air, or by satellites circling even higher. Waves all around the world might be predicted if this type of weather information could be put together quickly.

Learning to surf takes practice. A surfer must constantly adjust the body to keep control of the surfboard. A surfer's feet are also very important. The person does not stand still on the surfboard, but walks around the board, from nose to tail, from rail to rail. A surfer's head is important, too. The smallest movement of the head can cause enough movement in the rest of the body for a surfer to be thrown off balance. The proper use of one's arms are also important to maintain the balance necessary while surfing.

The two forms of "paddling out" are pictured above; (left) the surfer lies on his stomach, (right) shows the kneeling position.

Surfing is a very popular sport!

Riding the surf can be divided into four steps:

- paddling out to meet the waves
- the take-off
- the ride
- the pull-out.

Paddling out to the waves may sound easy, but it isn't. It is hard work. A surfer must be in good physical condition to paddle with ease.

There are two ways to paddle. A surfer can kneel or lie on his stomach on his surfboard. Learning to steer a board with ease is important whichever way you choose to paddle.

The surfer must paddle directly into each wave to get through it. It is important to stay out of the way of incoming surfers. The surfer must carefully paddle around the breaking surf when riders are in the area.

When the surfer first stands up on the board it is called a take off. This requires a great deal of practice.

First the surfer selects a wave. Then gives a strong kick with both legs to turn the board toward shore. Next, the board is paddled with a few strong strokes to get in motion with the wave. The surfer stands up as soon as the board begins sliding down the face of the wave.

Most surfers stand with their left foot forward on their boards. Those who stand with their right foot forward are called "goofy-footers."

A good surfer rides the steepest part of the wave. This is at the edge of the curl. The rider will be found farther down in the trough only if riding a hollow tube. By riding this part of the wave one will be able to keep the fin of the surfboard in the water.

Surfers ride across the face of the wave, almost parallel to the shore. They do not ride straight toward the shore.

Being able to keep the board in the correct spot on the wave with the right balance is called "trimming." A surfer must keep as much of the board touching the water as possible to keep it in "trim."

To turn, a surfer must make one side of the board slide faster than the other. This is done by shifting one's weight to make the desired turn.

A surfer walks toward the nose of the board to make it go faster. To stall or slow a board down, weight is shifted to the tail of the board. A rider must be careful not to stall too much. It will slow the surfer right out of a good ride.

eft foot forward is the position used by
ost surfers.

Right foot forward is a "goofy-footer"
surfer.

The pull-out is a very important part of the ride. Doing it correctly can prevent the loss of a surfboard and a long swim back to shore. A surfer must turn the board back into the wave to pull-out of a ride. There are many different ways to do this. It is up to each surfer to find the best. Many surfers raise the nose of the board high enough to clear the crest of the wave. Some surfers squat and go under the wave.

Surfers must be constantly alert to prevent a "wipe-out." It is called a "wipe-out" when a rider falls off his board.

Once a surfer has mastered the basics of riding the waves, two styles of surfing are practiced. One is the trick riding or hot-dogging. The other is the functional or classic surfing.

The "pull-out."

The surfer must turn the board back into the wave to "pull-out" of a ride.

Big waves attack the "classic" surfer.

A "hot-dogger" in action.

Hot-doggers ride the smaller waves and do tricks on their boards. The classic surfers look for bigger waves and try to get as much speed as possible. Hot-doggers often ride waves that are three to four feet high. Classic surfers may take on waves that are 15 to 20 feet high! Both styles of surfing take great skill and lots of practice.

Hot-doggers will try almost any trick possible while riding their boards. They stand on their heads and ride backwards. Sometimes they ride "tandem" with a partner on the same board. Tandem means two people riding on one board.

Hot-dogging goes back to the 1920's. One of the most famous hot-doggers was Dewey Weber, who was also an expert on skis. Many consider him the original hot-dogger and refer to him as the father of hot-dogging.

Dewey Weber the father of "hot-dog" surfing.

Today there are amateur and professional contests for both hot-doggers and classic surfers. The most famous is the International Surfing Championships held each winter at Makaha Beach, Hawaii. There are also contests in other parts of the United States, Australia, Japan, South Africa and Peru. France, Spain, Portugal and England have held surfing contests, too.

Most contests are sponsored by companies who make surfing equipment. They are organized and supported by the various surfing clubs.

Surfers must always be conscious of safety. The best rules are to stay alert and keep out of the way of other surfers. Anyone who tries to surf should be a good rough-water swimmer. Some surfing schools suggest that people should not try surfing unless they can swim at least 300 yards without stopping.

Probably the greatest danger in surfing is loose boards being tossed about by the waves. Skilled surfers who lose their balance should dive toward the waves grabbing their boards as they go. They should come up with their hands over their heads after a wipe-out. This helps prevent their own boards from hitting them in the head.

Skilled surfers must also watch out for cold water cramps. Like swimmers, they follow the safety rule of never surfing alone.

A wipe out!

Under the "curl."

Experienced surfers do not panic in a wipe-out. They do not fight the wave, but relax and let the action of the water release them. Then they swim for the top of the wave.

Surfers years ago taught themselves to ride the waves. Today's surfers have a variety of summertime camps and training schools to attend. Some high schools near the oceans also provide classes in surfing.

The sport is no longer reserved just for kings. Many ordinary men and women, young and old, enjoy it. Surfing is one of the most exciting water sports, and can be one of the most challenging. Would you like to try it on your next vacation? If you do, remember . . .
BIG WAVES CAN BE POWERFUL!

Sometimes the news people asked her about school and her life at home. They wanted to know what she thought about things like drugs. She told them that she had never even wanted to try drugs.

Back in school, Chris was still an honor student. She even found time to be editor of her high school yearbook. All this time she kept practicing every day. She also took time to help young players learn the game.

Chris takes time out to chat with young fans.

Chris graduated with her high school class in Fort Lauderdale in 1973. She had been waiting for her eighteenth birthday so she could turn pro. Many of her friends were going away to college. But she decided to be a professional tennis player.

Chris played her first pro tournament in the summer of 1973. She won $10,000. She bought presents for everyone in her family. "Being a pro is lots of fun," she said.

Chris was happy about winning, but she was not satisfied. She wanted to defeat top players. She said, "I just want someone to start testing me, someone to give me a real struggle."

Chris learns how it feels to lose.

Chris soon got her wish. She made the finals at the French Open. She lost to Margaret Court. Then she lost to Evonne Goolagong in the Italian Open. Virginia Wade defeated her at Nottingham. Julie Heldman beat her in England. After she lost, Chris did not want to call home to tell her father. Her mother was with her. She tried to comfort her. "It's good experience, Chrissie," she said.

Even when things did not go well, Chris did not lose her temper. She was known for being cool. For this reason some of her fans did not continue to support her. They thought she was too calm. Some writers wrote things that upset her. She told one reporter, "Don't wait for me to throw my racket. That just isn't me. And don't expect me to use bad words or clown around."

Margaret Court comforts Chris after a loss.

Chris plays Billie Jean King at Forest Hills.

One of the people who had noticed Chris was another top tennis player. His name was Jimmy Connors. He was very different from Chris. People thought they were too different to like each other. But Jimmy paid more and more attention to Chris. She liked him. Chris went to

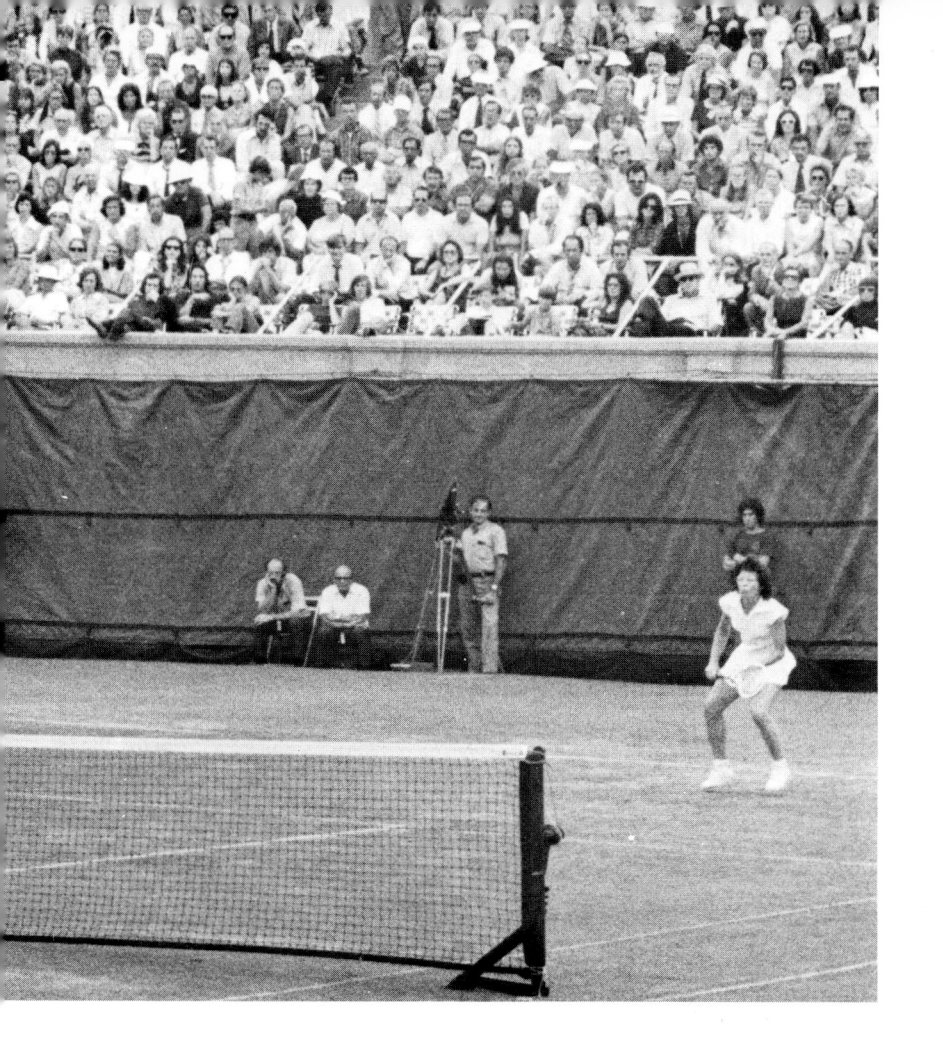

Wimbledon again. Jimmy Connors was there to watch. Chris made it to the semi-finals. She defeated Margaret Court. Then she played Billie Jean King. Billie Jean was a champion for women's rights. The crowd was for Bille Jean. She beat Chris 6-0, 7-5.

Chris came back to America after losing at Wimbledon. She was disappointed, but she had not lost her good nature. Back home, she began winning again. She won the Clay Courts title again. People began to say that no one could defeat her on a clay court.

Again Chris was on the U.S. team to win the Wightman Cup. Then she returned to Forest Hills. Chris really wanted to win at Forest Hills this year. She felt that she was ready. But it was not to be. She played in the semi-finals. But she lost to Margaret Court, 7-5, 2-6, 6-2.

This was the third time Chris had lost at Forest Hills. She began to work even harder. She improved her serve. She began to play a faster game of tennis. She also spent more time with Jimmy Connors. They played tennis together. They were seen together often. They began to talk about their future. Reporters began to write about their romance.

Jimmy Connors and Chris Evert spend time together on and off the court.

Chris and her friend Olga Morozova play a doubles match at Forest Hills.

1974 was a good year for Chris. Her game had improved. She was faster and stronger. First she won the singles championship at the Italian Open. Then she and her friend from Russia, Olga Morozova, won the doubles championship. The two of them played together in the French doubles. They won.

Chris and Jimmy after their Wimbledon victories.

Then it was back to Wimbledon. She made it to the finals. She had to play against her friend Olga. She defeated her Russian friend, 6-0, 6-4. Everyone could see that Chris was a strong champion.

Jimmy Connors also won at Wimbledon. The fans and news people were all talking about them. Everyone was taking pictures of them with their trophies. Chris and Jimmy had talked about marriage. But they were both busy with tournaments. Chris was the top woman player and Jimmy was the top man. Chris knew that if she got married she wanted to have a home and children. She had worked hard to become a great athlete. She said, "When you've done something all your life, when you've practiced hard and reached the top, it's not easy to quit." Chris and Jimmy decided not to get married.

1975 was another great year for Chris. She defeated Billie Jean King in the World Series of Women's Tennis. She lost to Billie Jean at Wimbledon. But she had won at Wimbledon in 1974. She was looking ahead to the match at Forest Hills. This was the one she had never won.

At the finals at Forest Hills, Chris was to play Evonne Goolagong. Evonne won the first set. Chris won the second. Then Chris won the third. She had won at Forest Hills! The U.S. Open was hers at last. At age twenty she had won the title that meant the most to her. It was her own national championship.

By the end of 1975, Chris was the top woman tennis player in the world. She had won more prize money than any other woman. She had won more than all the men except Jimmy Connors.

Between tournaments Chris had time to return home to be with her family. She did things she had not had time to do before. She liked to go to the beach with her younger brother John. She said, "You know something funny? As close as we are in my family, I've been so involved with tennis that I've missed much that many people take for granted. I've discovered how important my family really is to me, particularly my mom and dad."

Chris began to think more about her future. She knew that some day she would no longer be playing in tournaments. She started a company called Chrissie Evert for Puritan. Many girls had liked the tennis dresses she wore. They would be able to buy tennis outfits with Chris Evert's name on them.

Chris wears an 1874 design tennis dress for a costume pageant. Mrs. Evert helps with the finishing touches.

This did not mean that Chris was quitting tennis. She still practiced to improve her skills. She practiced with her father every day. She was never satisfied.

In 1976 Chris played in more tournaments. She played well in the Virginia Slims Tournament in Los Angeles. But Evonne Goolagong played better. Evonne won the first set. Chris won the second. Then Evonne won the third. The fans seemed to favor Evonne. It seemed that Chris had won too many times. After all, she had won $703,262 in just three years.

After the match, Chris showed what a great sport she was. Evonne had played better than ever to beat Chris. Chris said, "I think Evonne has become more consistent, that's why I was able to defeat her before, by trying to out-steady her. But you can't outsteady her anymore. Her good strokes are so good. So I think I'm going to have to develop a better net game and a better serve."

She did, too. At Wimbledon Chris beat Evonne 6-3, 4-5, 8-6. She regained the title she lost in 1975.

In 1976, ninety-six women were trying to win the crown at Forest Hills. This year the U.S. Open contest would be on TV for many people to see. More and more people were interested in tennis. More people were playing tennis themselves. Everyone was talking about who would win. One writer said, "Anyone who bets against Evert has to be rich, reckless, or both." Another said, "Evert played a great final to win last year, the surface is hers." Still another said, "Evert is the finest clay-court player in the history of the game." Others said simply, "Evert will win."

The pressure was on Chris to keep her title. The final match between Chris and Evonne took place before a crowd of 16,244 people. The *New York Times* the next day said, "Miss Evert won, 6-3, 6-0 and retained her title."

Chris Evert had won the U.S. Open again. Many people said that she was the greatest the world had ever seen - male or female. She had won 100 clay court matches in a row. She had won the Virginia Slims championship three times in four years. She had lost only five matches over the season. She had brought home titles from San Francisco, Akron, and Houston. She was the first player in history to win individual events of the Triple Crown of Women's Tennis.

In 1977 and 1978 Chris continued to be the number one woman player. Although she didn't win at Wimbledon, she won the U.S. Open both years. After winning the U.S. Indoor's title in 1978, *Sports Illustrated* magazine selected her "Sportswoman of the Year."

1979 was another story. It was Chris's worst year since she became a pro. Martina Navratilova beat her for the second year in a row in the Wimbledon finals, and Tracy Austin beat her in the U.S. Open finals. She lost 15 matches in all during the year. After five year's as the top American player, she dropped to number two.

A bright spot in this bad year was Chris's marriage to British tennis player, John Lloyd. They were married in Fort Lauderdale, Florida on April 17, 1979. It was a very happy time for Chris and her family.

Chris gets a kiss from her father, Jimmy Evert.

After a disappointing loss to Evonne Goolagong in the 1980 Wimbledon finals (6-1, 7-6), Chris decided to quit playing tennis for awhile. She wanted time to think about her game. Tennis fans missed her at tournaments and they wondered if she would play again.

By the end of the summer Chris felt that she was ready to play. She decided to enter the 1980 U.S. Open at Forest Hills.

At first, it seemed that Chris was right. She easily defeated everyone in the opening rounds, and got to the finals.

Her opponent in the finals was Hana Mandlikova, a young star from Czechoslovakia. Hana won the first set 7-5, and many fans were worried that Chris would not regain her title after all.

But Chris came roaring back and Hana lost control. Chris won the next two sets 6-1, 6-1. The U.S. Open title was hers once more!

In the hearts and minds of almost everyone, Chris Evert Lloyd was again the best woman tennis player in the world.

If You Enjoyed

CHRIS EVERT LLOYD
WOMEN'S TENNIS CHAMPION

Then Don't Miss Reading

MUHAMMAD ALI
THE GREATEST

O. J. SIMPSON
THE JUICE IS LOOSE

EVEL KNIEVEL
MOTORCYCLE DAREDEVIL

DOROTHY HAMILL
SKATE TO VICTORY

FRAN TARKENTON
MASTER OF THE GRIDIRON

from

CRESTWOOD HOUSE

P.O. BOX 3427   MANKATO, MINNESOTA 56001

Write Us for a Complete Catalog